A Time in My
Autobiographical V

Selected by Wendy Bo

Contents

Section 1: Work and Play

Cookie – a Dedication — 2
from *My Life in Dog Years* by Gary Paulsen

School Days — 8
from *A Kind of Magic* by Mollie Harris

Section 2: In Time of War

The Shop — 13
from *War Boy* by Michael Foreman

June 1942 and April 1944 — 18
from *The Diary of Anne Frank*

Section 3: At Sea

Voyage to Australia 1883 — 22
from an unpublished journal by William Collis

Into the Lifeboat — 28
from *Titanic Survivor, The Memoirs of Violet Jessop*

Edinburgh Gate
Harlow, Essex

Cookie – a Dedication

Gary Paulsen wrote this piece as an introduction to his book My Life in Dog Years …

Though I ran sled dogs for close to ten years, did some twenty-two thousand miles with them, this book is not about sled dogs or running them. They were truly wonderful and I have written of them in other books. This book is about other dogs in my life and other times. I am – I say this with some pride and not a little wonder – a 'dog person'. I make no excuses for unabashedly loving them – all of them, even some that have bitten me. I have always had dogs and will have dogs until I die. I have rescued dozens of dogs from pounds, always have five or six of them around me, and cannot imagine living without dogs. They are wonderful and, I think, mandatory for decent human life.

All that said, there are some dogs that are different, special in amazing ways.

Cookie was my lead dog when I first started to run dogs, and she was also my lead dog in my first Iditarod sled dog race; she took me from Anchorage to Nome, Alaska, when most people – including me – thought I couldn't do it.

But she was more. She was a good friend, a kind of dogsister or dogmother to me, and while I have written much of her in other places, she belongs in this book, too.

Cookie was given to me by a man who thought she was so sick she couldn't run any longer. She merely had worms, and when I wormed her she became a wonderful sled dog, and then a wonderful lead dog.

I did not set out to race dogs; I used them for work. I brought in wood with them, went to the Laundromat in town with them (it was grand to tie the dogs up to the parking meter and watch people jump as they walked by) and trapped with them.

In January of 1980 I was running a seventy-five mile line, trapping beaver. I had previously trapped with a friend, but this year I was trapping alone, not the wisest thing to do, since there is some risk from bad ice or injuries and it's better to have a companion. I was alone when I made a mistake that nearly killed me.

The ice around beaver lodges is very dangerous. Beavers live in their lodges and come out of underwater tunnels to get food they have stored at the bottom of the river or pond through the summer, in the form of branches stuck down in the mud. Each time they come out they let air out of their noses and it goes up to make bubbles under the surface of the ice, and this, along with the beavers' rubbing their backs on the underside of the ice, keeps the ice very thin near a beaver lodge. It can be fifty below with two-foot-thick ice around the whole lake and the ice near the lodge might be less than a quarter inch thick.

I had parked the sled near a lodge and unpacked the gear needed to set a group of snares. Cookie was leading the work team of five dogs and they knew the procedure completely by this time. As soon as I stopped the sled and began to unpack they all lay down, curled their tails over their noses and went to sleep. The process could take two or three hours and they used the time to rest.

A rope tied the cargo to the sled. I threw the rope across the ice to get it out of the way. One end was still tied to the sled. I took a step on the ice near the rope and went through and down like a stone.

You think there is time to react, that the ice will give way slowly and you'll be able to hang on to the edge, somehow able to struggle to safety. It's not that way at all. It's as if you were suddenly standing on air. The bottom drops out and you go down.

I was wearing heavy clothing and a parka. It gathered water like a sponge and took me down faster.

Two things saved me. One, as I went down my hand fell across the rope I had thrown across the ice, which was still tied to the sled.

Two, as I dropped I had time to yell – scream – and the last thing I saw as I went under was Cookie's head swinging up from sleeping and her eyes locking on mine as I went beneath the surface.

The truth is I shouldn't have lived. I have had several friends killed in just this manner – dropping through the ice while running dogs – and there wasn't much of a chance for me. The water was ten or twelve feet deep. I saw all the bubbles from my clothing going up to the surface and I tried to pull myself up on the rope. My hands slipped and I thought in a wild, mental scream of panic that this was how it would end.

Then the rope tightened. There was a large noose-knot on the end and it tightened and started pulling up and when the knot hit I grabbed and held and the dogs pulled me out of the hold and back

up onto the ice. There was still very little time. I had a quart of white-gas stove fuel on the sled for emergencies and I threw it on a pine tree nearby and lit a match and set the whole tree on fire and, in the heat, got my clothes off and crawled into a sleeping bag. I stood inside it and held my clothes near the flame to dry them.

I would have died if not for Cookie.

She saw me drop, instantly analysed the situation, got the team up – she must have jerked them to their feet – got them pulling, and they pulled me out.

That was January 1980. It is now 1997 as I write this, and everything that has happened in the last seventeen years – everything: Iditarods, published books, love, living, life – all of it, including this book, I owe to Cookie.

**From *My Life in Dog Years*
by Gary Paulsen**

School Days

Mollie Harris was one of seven children in her family. Her book, A Kind of Magic, *is written for adults and describes growing up in the Oxfordshire village of Ducklington in the 1920s. Here, she remembers games at school …*

At school, boys and girls played together in a small playground where there were four bucket lavatories for the girls and four for the boys, separated by sheets of corrugated iron. The boys used to try to frighten the girls in all sorts of ways, and once one of them put a great hedgehog in a newly emptied bucket. Then they waited for the first girl to go in.

It happened to be a timid, rather shy girl and fairly new to the school. She saw the animal just as she was about to sit down and, letting out a loud scream, came rushing out with her long, white, lace-edged drawers hanging round her knees. Then they fell to her ankles and she went headlong, full length onto the hard playground. The screaming and shouting brought out Mr Preston and all the boys got six of the best.

● ● ●

There was no special time to start certain games. For weeks we all might be skipping madly, then one day someone would come to school with a bag of marbles or a whip and top, and suddenly all the other children did the same …

Of course, marbles was a summer craze, a slower, quieter game, and if you had a penny you could buy twenty chalk marbles. A Tally, which was the one you scattered the smaller ones with, usually cost a farthing and was often made of clear glass with bright, multi-coloured wavy threads in. If you were lucky enough to find an empty lemonade bottle that had been thrown away, a sharp crack on a stone broke the bottle and released a super glass Tally for nothing. Boys *and* girls played the game, but it was really considered more of a boy's game. The marbles were carried around in flannel bags secured tightly at the top with a thread of tape.

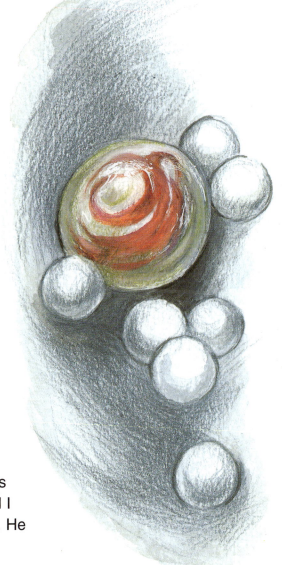

Once, from somewhere, I'd got four marbles and a glass Tally and one night after school I plagued the champion of the village to play. He was a big bully of a lad and sniggered as I challenged him.

"I shall take your few fust game, you see if I dun't! Hark at 'er challenging I, thur yent nobody in the school as can beat I."

It was true too, and he and his followers used to walk to the other villages and challenge the kids there.

"Set 'um up then Mollie, we en't got long to 'ang about yer, we be awf up to Witney tu beat some a they tonight." We placed our marbles on the dusty road against the school wall.

"You go fust," Bert said, "cost if you dun't you wun't 'ave no chance at all tu play."

I took careful aim and scattered the row of chalk marbles.

"Coo!" one of the other boys said, "that was a lucky aim." I quickly picked up my winnings.

"Beginner's luck – thas what that was," Bert sniggered. He stood well back, took aim at the fresh row we had set up – and missed!

"Crikey! Wass up wi you?" Percy Russell said. "Strikes I you be nervous Bert."

For the next half hour we played and Bert the Bully never won a game. The other boys were shouting and cheering me on and Bert was swearing and getting redder and redder. Then it came to the pitch when he set his last few marbles in a row. Spitting on his hands he swore he'd beat me yet. But he didn't, and mad with temper he flung his super lucky Tally at me, hitting me sharply in the face.

"There, take that!" he said. "I'll win 'um all back tomorrow, you see if I dun't." Then he and his gang moved off, shouting and swearing. I stuffed my winnings into Bert's flannel marble bag that he'd left lying on the ground and ran off home.

When I got to school next morning Bert and his gang were bowling their iron hoops in the playground.

"En't you going tu try and win 'um back?" I asked, clutching my bag of marbles.

"No I blumen well en't," he said. "Shove off. Marbles is a girl's game," and they tore away and charged round the playground like a herd of young bullocks. In fact nobody wanted to play. They were all too busy bowling their hoops.

**From *A Kind of Magic*
by Mollie Harris**

The Shop

Our mother ran the village shop. She sold everything, from sweets to sealing wax and string. The pavement outside was piled high with vegetables. Inside, the shop always seemed full of legs. Khaki legs, sailors' legs, busmen's legs and, worst of all, little old ladies' legs. I had a horror of being trapped under voluminous dark skirts smelling of rotten lavender and cats' pee.

Our home and shop stood with two other little houses on a kind of triangular traffic island surrounded by three roads. It was at the end of the bus route from town, and after turning the buses around, the drivers and conductors had five minutes' break.

Mother made tea in a great big pot, and the busmen drank it from saucers as they couldn't wait for it to cool.

The soldiers and sailors had more time. They stood about the shop and joked and told stories while they drank their tea, saucer in one hand, cup in the other and a ciggy smouldering between two fingers. Often they filled the shop and spilled out onto the pavement. Ordinary customers, old men coming for their tobacco and old ladies doing their bits of shopping, had to push their way through the throng. Younger ladies didn't seem to mind the crush and enjoyed the jokes I didn't understand.

All the young local men were away, in uniforms, drinking tea and getting shot at some place else.

One day, the scream of a falling bomb sent everyone in the shop diving into a heap on the floor. Tea everywhere. The house of Mr Lang, the chemist just up the road, was destroyed.

We had no garden. The tiny yard at the back was filled with sacks of potatoes, carrots and turnips. Even our big tin bath on the coal bunker was full of cabbages and cauliflowers from one Saturday bath night to the next.

The shop, then, was the playground of my toddler years. That the shop was perpetually full of soldiers and sailors seemed quite normal to me. In 1940 the whole world seemed full of soldiers and sailors. It was fun crawling in and out of their legs, while they stood among the sacks of veg and drank tea and joked. It was educational too. I learned very colourful language. This I directed at any approaching old lady's legs.

The men decided this child needed discipline. I was drilled every morning. Dressed either as a soldier or sailor, depending on who was to be Drill Sergeant, I was inspected in the shop, then marched up and down the pavement while massed ranks of tea drinkers shouted, "Left Right, Left Right, About Turn, Pick Them Feet Up!"

A village shop window, stuffed full, with nothing costing more than a penny (you could ask for a penn'orth of anything) is a sight no child can pass. The children of Pakefield were poor. A penny to spend was a rare treat. The spending required a lot of thought and took a lot of time. The penny was spent many times over in the imagination as they peered over the boxes of veg outside the shop at the rows of glass jars at the back of the window.

Pear drops, humbugs, fruit drops, liquorice comforts, gob-stoppers. You got more pear drops for a penny, but you might have to share them with your little brother or sister, or any of the notorious *Botwright* brothers if you happened to meet one in a back opening. Gob-stoppers last longer and you were less likely to have to share (although half-sucked gob-stoppers were often passed round, usually from my pocket and then mouth to mouth through the Botwright hierarchy).

Liquorice comforts were most fun. They were sucked slowly until only the black centre remained. This stained all your teeth black. If you were careful you could blacken only a few, or every other one. Earlier in the sucking stage, while there was still colour on the comforts, you could war-paint yourself and several other members of the gang in the full range of candy colours. Psychedelia came early to the Hill Green Gang.

Now, it was my good fortune, as a toddler, to be placed in the middle of this Aladdin's Cave of penny treasures. The only place safe from the feet of busmen and the Allies, and where my mother could keep an eye on me, was in the shop window. Also, away from the dark threat of their skirts, I was less likely to be rude to old ladies.

This was my window on the world. A window criss-crossed with anti-blast sticky tape, but a window which burnt penny-sized holes in the pockets of children in the street. A window past which swirled the machinery of war, the baker's horse-drawn van, the brewers' drays, and Stewey White, the tipsy coalman whose horse took him home every night.

Every ten minutes or so a bus crew would arrive for their five-minute break. They liked it 'hot 'n' strong'.

At one end of the glass counter was a big wooden bakers' tray, full of very dull-looking cakes. Some had a fingerprint of jam on top to suggest memories of a cherry. Others had a little black currant on top. If you saw a cake with two currants, one of them would be a fly.

Sitting in the shop window in summer was not without danger. Any bruised fruit attracted swarms of wasps. The wasps would gorge

themselves for a while, then climb with sticky feet part way up the window and doze off in the sun. Boys outside the window would pretend to lick them off, or drum on the glass with their fingers and stir the wasps up into such a fury that they would dive-bomb the closely packed tea-swilling customers.

I don't think I was ever stung, despite having the stickiest face and fingers in the village.

**From *War Boy*
by Michael Foreman**

June 1942 and April 1944

Anne Frank was a Jewish girl who went into hiding with her family to escape the Nazis during the Second World War. Before they went into hiding in July 1942 Anne wrote:

Saturday, 20th June 1942

I haven't written for a few days, because I wanted first of all to think about my diary. It's an odd idea for someone like me to keep a diary; not only because I have never done so before, but because it seems to me that neither I – nor for that matter anyone else – will be interested in the unbosomings of a thirteen-year-old schoolgirl. Still, what does that matter? I want to write, but more than that, I want to bring out all kinds of things that lie buried deep in my heart.

There is a saying that 'paper is more patient than man'; it came back to me on one of my slightly melancholy days, while I sat chin in hand, feeling too bored and limp even to make up my mind whether to go out or to stay at home. Yes, there is no doubt that paper is patient and as I don't intend to show this cardboard-covered notebook, bearing the proud name of 'diary', to anyone, unless I find a real friend, boy or girl, probably nobody cares. And now I come to the root of the matter, the reason for my starting a diary: it is that I have no such real friend …

Hence, this diary. In order to enhance in my mind's eye the picture of the friend for whom I have waited so long, I don't want to set down a series of bald facts in a diary like most people do, but I want this diary itself to be my friend, and I shall call my friend Kitty …

Tuesday, 4th April 1944

Dear Kitty,

For a long time I haven't had any idea of what I was working for any more; the end of the war is so terribly far away, so unreal, like a fairy tale. If the war isn't over by September I shan't go to school any more. Because I don't want to be two years behind. Peter filled my days – nothing but Peter, in dreams and thoughts until Saturday, when I felt so utterly miserable; oh, it was terrible. I was holding back my tears all the while I was with Peter, then laughed with Van Daan over a lemon-punch, was cheerful and excited, but the moment I was alone I knew that I would have to cry my heart out. So, clad in my nightdress, I let myself go and slipped down onto the floor. First I said my long prayer very earnestly, then I cried with my head on my arms, my knees bent up, on the bare floor, completely folded up. One large sob brought me back to earth again, and I quelled my tears because I didn't want them to hear anything in the next room. Then I began trying to talk some courage into myself. I could only say: "I must, I must, I must …"

Completely stiff from the unnatural position I fell against the side of the bed and fought on, until I climbed into bed again just before half-past ten. It was over!

And now it's all over. I must work, so as not to be a fool, to get on, to become a journalist, because that's what I want! I know that I can write, a couple of my stories are good, my descriptions of the 'Secret Annexe' are humorous, there's a lot in my diary that speaks, but – whether I have real talent remains to be seen.

'Eva's Dream' is my best fairy-tale, and the queer thing about it is that I don't know where it comes from. Quite a lot of 'Cady's Life' is good too, but, on the whole, it's nothing. I am the best and sharpest critic of my own work.

I know myself what is and what is not well written. Anyone who doesn't write doesn't know how wonderful it is; I used to bemoan the fact that I couldn't draw at all, but now I am more than happy that I can at least write. And if I haven't any talent for writing books or newspaper articles, well, then I can always write for myself.

I want to get on; I can't imagine that I would have to lead the same sort of life as Mummy and Mrs Van Daan and all the women who do their work and are then forgotten. I must have something besides a husband and children, something that I can devote myself to!

I want to go on living even after my death! And therefore I am grateful to God for giving me this gift, this possibility of developing myself and of writing, of expressing all that is in me.

I can shake off everything if I write; my sorrows disappear, my courage is reborn. But, and that is the great question, will I ever be able to write anything great, will I ever become a journalist or a writer? I hope so, I hope so very much, for I can recapture everything when I write, my thoughts, my ideas and my fantasies.

I haven't done anything more to 'Cady's Life' for ages; in my mind I know exactly how to go on, but somehow it doesn't flow from my pen. Perhaps I never shall finish it, it may land up in the wastepaper basket, or the fire … that's a horrible idea, but then I think to myself, 'at the age of fourteen and with so little experience, how can you write about philosophy?'

So I go on again with fresh courage; I think I shall succeed, because I want to write!

Yours,

Anne

Anne Frank died of typhus in a Nazi concentration camp in March 1945. Since her diary was published in 1947, it has been read by millions of people throughout the world.

From *The Diary of Anne Frank*

Voyage to Australia 1883

> *These extracts come from an old diary written by my great uncle, William Collis. At the age of 20 he went to Australia with his brother and 340 other emigrants. He stayed in Australia for a few years, working and gold prospecting. He came back to England to be married and died later in 1934.*
>
> Wendy Body

Saturday, September 15th

At five o'clock on the morning of the fifteenth of September Eighteen Eighty Three, we were awoke by the sailors who were busy weighing the anchor, at the same time singing the anchor shanty. We were all very soon on deck, lending them a helping hand. As soon as the anchor was up and made fast to the cathead, a hauser was passed out to a steam tug which was waiting alongside and made fast to her, she then started tugging us out to sea.

The morning was foggy so we soon lost sight of old England. Everyone seemed quite jolly, with the exception of a few females, who added a little more water to the briny deep, thinking there was not enough to sail our ship. We passed by the noble Eddystone, there are some awful dangerous rocks round it.

The steam tug left us about one mile south of the Eddystone lighthouse, then the sails were unfurled, the anchors weighed.

'Farewell, farewell,' was sung by some of the young men, after which, we went below with a good appetite.

There was scarcely a breeze of wind blowing all day, so we made but little progress towards getting over the sixteen thousand miles which are now before us. The day passed very pleasantly, as everything was new to us landlubbers, we sighted a vessel in the channel, after which they were few and far between. The ship was very steady, so we didn't feel sick in the least.

Monday, September 17th

Weather stormy, strong breeze blowing.

The *SS Sydenham* measures two hundred and twenty feet long, thirty-eight feet wide, forty feet from the keel to the main deck and one hundred and ninety feet from the main deck to the top of the main mast. The crew consists of twenty-six able and ordinary seamen, this being a double crew to what they would have if they had no passengers. Boatswain, Carpenter, Sailmaker, Engineer, First, Second and Third Mates, Two Stewards, Two Cooks, One Baker and Alexander Ross the Captain. The *Sydenham* carries six life boats, each boat having a keg of fresh water in case we are wrecked.

Our vessel pitched and rolled today for the first time, which made most of us begin casting up our accounts; it was amusing to see all of us hanging our heads over the bulwarks, shooting the cat. Many a bitter curse the sailors gave us today, they had all their work cut out to keep the decks clean. We stayed on deck till late at night.

Wednesday, November 21st

Weather wet, fair wind.

We had a very heavy storm in the night. The main top gallant, the fore top gallant and one stay sail was carried away. We were obliged to stay below for fear of being washed overboard, tons of water were sweeping her decks from stem to stern, every moment we thought we were going under. It was a fearful rough night, the vessel shook and trembled as though she would break in pieces.

A child was born in the night.

We were running before a gale of wind all night long.

Thursday, December 6th

Weather rough, head wind.

The wind was blowing a hurricane all day. We made but little progress as it was a head wind.

Another terrific storm in the night, the fore top stay sail was carried away, it sounded like the report of a cannon. The sailors could not find out which one it was till morning as it was so dark, when they found a few rags of sail left.

A child died in the night.

Tuesday, December 11th

Weather fine, calm.

A school of whales round our vessel spouting, it looked like a lot of fountains playing. A large one came close to the bows of our vessel, he came to the top, spouted, then gave a grunt and disappeared. He smelled very oily and measured between thirty and forty feet.

Six albatross caught today, the largest measured 11 ft 6 ins across the wings.

Child buried this afternoon.

Tuesday, December 25th

Christmas Day.

"Land ahead," was shouted by the man on the look out at break of day. It passed through the vessel like an electric shock and in a few minutes we were all straining our eyes to see the long promised land. The officers were all busy taking soundings, they had to stop the ship because she was running straight for land. We saw the light from Sydney lighthouse as it revolved, we were then about seventy miles from Sydney.

We sailed along in sight of land till eleven a.m. when we were opposite the Heads, which are two high rocks, one on each side of the harbour mouth. The Captain then signalled for a tug which we soon saw coming towards us, also another steamer which was bringing a pilot who was soon on our vessel. A cord was thrown to the tug boat with a hauser attached to it which was soon made fast to the tug and then we soon found ourselves in Sydney Harbour.

We dropped anchor in the quarantine quarters for inspection. After dinner a doctor came on board to examine us. He found us all well and healthy, with the exception of two children who had the whooping cough, for which we have to stay in quarantine for four days.

It was a lovely day and we had a splendid view around us, in fact we were completely shut in from the Pacific. The harbour was full of mackerel it being the season for them here, so we amused ourselves fishing.

We had a very happy Christmas, finishing with a concert on the quarter deck. The harbour was full of pleasure boats decked with flags and flowers.

From an unpublished journal by William Collis

Into the Lifeboat

Violet Jessop worked at sea and made over 200 voyages. Aged 25, she was a stewardess on the Titanic *when it sank on its maiden voyage in April 1912. She finished writing her memoirs in 1934 and died in 1970. Violet's memoirs were published in 1997 at the wish of her family.*

You could almost imagine this a scene of busily curious people with not very much to do. True, there were officers and men briskly getting lifeboats ready to lower, their tense faces strangely in contrast to the well ordered groups wandering about. I felt chilly without a coat, so I went down again for something to cover my shoulders and picked up a silk eiderdown from the first cabin I came to. How strange it was to pass all those rooms lit up so brilliantly, their doors open and contents lying around in disorder. Jewels sparkled on dressing tables and a pair of silver slippers were lying just where they had been kicked off.

I gathered my eiderdown and went up. On my way I passed a group of officers, still in their mess jackets, hands in pockets, chatting quietly on the companion square as men do who are waiting for something. They smiled at me and I waved back.

As I turned I ran into Jock, the bandleader and his crowd with their instruments. 'Funny, they must be going to play,' thought I, 'and at this late hour!' Jock smiled in passing, looking rather pale for him, remarking, "Just going to give them a tune to cheer things up a bit," and passed on. Presently the strains of the band reached me faintly as I stood on deck watching a young woman excitedly remonstrating with an embarrassed young officer. He wanted her to get into the lifeboat he was trying to fill but she refused to go without her father.

"He must wait," responded the officer, "till the decks are cleared of women and children."

• • •

We touched the water with a terrific thud, a bone-cracking thud which started the baby crying in earnest. Somebody in the forepart ordered oars out and we slowly pulled away from the side of the ship. I noticed one of the few men in the boat rowing; he was a fireman who had evidently just come up from the stokehold, his face still black with coal dust and eyes red-rimmed, wearing only a thin singlet to protect him from the icy cold. Taking a cigarette from his trouser pocket, he offered me half, poor devil!

Fascinated, my eyes never left the ship, as if by looking I could keep her afloat. I reflected that but four days ago I had wished to see her from afar, to be able to admire her under way; now there she was, my *Titanic*, magnificent queen of the ocean, a perfection of man's handiwork, her splendid lines outlined against the night, every light twinkling.

I started unconsciously to count the decks by the rows of lights. One, two, three, four, five, six; then again – one, two, three, four, five. I stopped. Surely I had miscounted. I went over them again more carefully, hushing the whimpering baby meanwhile.

No, I had made no mistake. There were only five decks now; then I started all over again – only four now. She was getting lower in the water, I could not any longer deny it.

As if all could read my mind, the women in the boat started to weep, some silently, some unrestrainedly. I closed my eyes and prayed, prayed for one and all but dared not think of anyone in particular. I dared not visualise those people I had just left, warm and alive as I was. I tried to busy myself with the baby, but could not refrain from looking up again. Only three decks now, and still not a list to one side or the other.

Desperately, I turned to where that other ship's lights shone on the horizon; surely they should be getting nearer by now. It was such a long, long time since we had first seen their comforting glow. They should be with us by now, taking off those patient waiting people over there. But no, she did not seem nearer, in fact, she seemed further away. Strange!

A tiny breeze, the first we had felt on this calm night, blew an icy blast across my face; it felt like a knife in its penetrating coldness. I sat paralysed with cold and misery, as I watched *Titanic* give a lurch forward. One of the huge funnels toppled off like a cardboard model, falling into the sea with a fearful roar. A few cries came to us across the water, then silence, as the ship seemed to right herself like a hurt animal with a broken back. She settled for a few minutes, but one more deck of lighted ports disappeared. Then she went down by the head with a thundering roar of underwater explosions, our proud ship, our beautiful *Titanic* gone to her doom.

One awful moment of empty, misty blackness enveloped us in its loneliness, then an unforgettable, agonising cry went up from 1500 despairing throats, a long wail and then silence and our tiny craft tossing about at the mercy of the ice field.

From *Titantic Survivor, The Memoirs of Violet Jessop*

ECO-FRIENDLY LIVING

KATIE DICKER

First published in Great Britain in 2021 by Wayland

Copyright © Hodder and Stoughton Limited, 2021

Produced for Wayland by
White-Thomson Publishing Ltd
www.wtpub.co.uk

All rights reserved.

Editor: Katie Dicker
Series Designer: Rocket Design (East Anglia) Ltd
Consultant: Dr Sharon George

HB ISBN: 978 1 5263 1524 3
PB ISBN: 978 1 5263 1525 0

Wayland
An imprint of
Hachette Children's Group
Part of Hodder & Stoughton
Carmelite House
50 Victoria Embankment
London EC4Y 0DZ

An Hachette UK Company
www.hachettechildrens.co.uk

Printed in China

Picture acknowledgements:
Alamy: Kevin Britland / Alamy Stock Photo 7b; American Chemical Society 21b; Blue Planet Ltd reference for 9b; Cambridge Consultants 22bl and 31; Getty: Abscent84 3t and 23tr, Medesulda 3b and 24m, bagrovskam 4, IngaNielsen 5b, DrAfter123 6, sompong_tom 16t, Youst 17, Goran13 19bl, Jason Finn 25t, elenabs 26–27b and 32, Tempura 27t, Pixtum 28t, Jon Wightman 28b; ©MIT/AMS Institute 27br; Shutterstock: SkyPics Studio cover tl, title bl and 10–11, petovarga cover tr, title tr, 24b and 30b, metamorworks cover ml, 7t and 26m, Mary Long cover m and title tl, Yauhen 44 cover mr, Lucky clover cover bl, Evgenia.B cover bm, Macrovector cover br, title br and 14, Siberian Art 2 and 21t, laymanzoom 5t, pathdoc 8, Zakharchenko Anna 11t, Boris Bulychev 12b, vectortatu 12ml, Mascha Tace 12mr, Vectorpocket 13t, Sketchbook Designs 15tr, Borisovstudio 15b, jossnat 16b, extripod 18m, Julia Tim 19tr, Lemberg Vector studio 20, Oceloti 23b, shaineast 25b, Abugrafie 29t; Smart Cups 18bl; University of Colorado Boulder College of Engineering and Applied Science 9t; WTE Ltd reference for 13b; www.collectors2020.eu reference for 19br; www.sdwforall.com 29b.

All design elements from Shutterstock or drawn by designer.

Every effort has been made to clear copyright. Should there be any inadvertent omission, please apply to the publisher for rectification.

The website addresses (URLs) included in this book were valid at the time of going to press. However, it is possible that contents or addresses may have changed since the publication of this book. No responsibility for any such changes can be accepted by either the author or the publisher.

All facts and statistics were correct at the time of press.

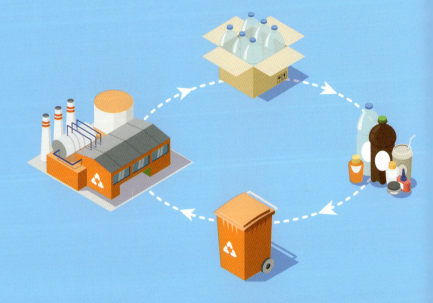

CONTENTS

What is eco-friendly living?	4
Renewable energy	6
Building our world	8
Smart homes	10
Water world	12
Clothes and fashion	14
Feeding the world	16
Packaging and parcels	18
Working with plastic	20
Waste and recycling	22
Getting around	24
Smart cities	26
Sustainable development	28
Glossary	30
Further information	31
Index	32

WHAT IS ECO-FRIENDLY LIVING?

Every day, the world's population grows by over 200,000 people and we're using more resources than ever before. Our activities are causing Earth's climate to get dangerously warmer. To limit our impact on Earth, we need to make some changes.

LOOKING AHEAD

For a long time, we didn't know quite how much damage we were causing and the consequences of the way we used Earth's resources. But when scientists noticed changes in Earth's climate, it became clear we had a serious problem. The gradual rise in Earth's temperature is putting our planet and the life within it at risk. We are polluting our environment and slowly running out of natural resources.

Planet Earth has the right conditions for life, but its future is in our hands.

PROTECTING EARTH

Eco-friendly living is about reducing the impact we have on our planet. It is something we can all do – from the food we eat to the clothes we wear, and the way we travel around. Governments play an important part, too. Regulations ensure that new buildings are designed to be eco-friendly for example (see page 8), and improved public transport helps to reduce pollution.

Green technology supports our efforts to make changes to our modern lifestyles.

Earth Overshoot Day

Earth Overshoot Day is the day we use up a year's worth of natural resources (the amount that Earth can regenerate in a year). In 1970, it was 29 December. In 2019, it was 29 July! We can't go on like this forever.

POWERFUL TECH

If we all make changes in our own lives, together we can make a big difference. Thankfully, some amazing technology is helping to speed up the process. Green tech has provided ways to use Earth's resources more efficiently. It has opened up non-polluting sources of energy and is helping poorer parts of the world to develop in an eco-friendly way. But it's also important that we continue to protect our natural world, rather than relying on technology to clean up our mess.

RENEWABLE ENERGY

For many years, we've used non-renewable resources to produce energy. Fossil fuels such as coal and oil, for example, will eventually run out. They also create harmful gases when they're burned. Scientists have developed renewable sources of energy that are cleaner and won't run out.

There are sources of energy all around us. We can tap into the power of the Sun, wind, water and Earth's natural heat.

NATURAL POWER

Renewable sources of energy use the power of nature. For example, the strength of the wind or of flowing water can turn a turbine to spin a generator and create electricity. The energy in sunlight can be captured to heat and power our homes. Earth's natural heat can warm water, and plant or animal waste can be used for fuel.

LESS CARBON

Scientists talk about carbon emissions or our 'carbon footprint' (the amount of carbon produced by an activity). This refers mainly to 'carbon dioxide' but also includes other greenhouse gases that warm our planet. An increase of these gases in our atmosphere traps more of the Sun's heat than is healthy for Earth. Renewable energy reduces this growing pollution and preserves resources.

CHANGING BEHAVIOUR

It can be difficult to change people's behaviour, but knowledge is often the key. Technology can now monitor our 'personal carbon footprint', for example, to find out the impact of the energy we're using. This knowledge can help us to make small changes to our lifestyles, creating new habits that bring us benefits (such as saving money) while also helping to save the planet.

Knowing our energy use can help us to make informed choices about our daily activities.

DID YOU KNOW?

The Sun's energy can now be used to power ovens, run air conditioning units, power streetlights and charge electronic devices. Scientists are currently developing cars that use solar power to recharge their batteries.

SOLAR POWER

As technology improves, it becomes easier to make changes at home, especially when governments subsidise eco-friendly tech (that is, make it cheaper for people to buy). For example, many more homes in the USA, Germany and Italy now use solar panels on roofs and in glass 'solar panel' skylights. Energy and resources are needed to make solar panels, but once in place, they can power homes and other buildings in sunny climates.

New roofs can be made from 'solar shingle tiles' – small solar panels that look like traditional roof tiles.

BUILDING OUR WORLD

We all need houses and places to work, but we need to reduce the impact that new buildings have on our planet. Manufacturing building materials, transporting them to building sites and the construction process itself, produces nearly 11 per cent of annual carbon emissions.

FEWER EMISSIONS

The construction of eco-friendly buildings produces fewer polluting gases. Instead of using cement and steel, wood has become a popular choice (and is long-lasting if well maintained). Trees absorb carbon dioxide from the air and store it safely in their trunks, so sustainable forests can reduce greenhouse gases while also providing a useful building material. If wood is grown locally, less fuel is needed to transport it.

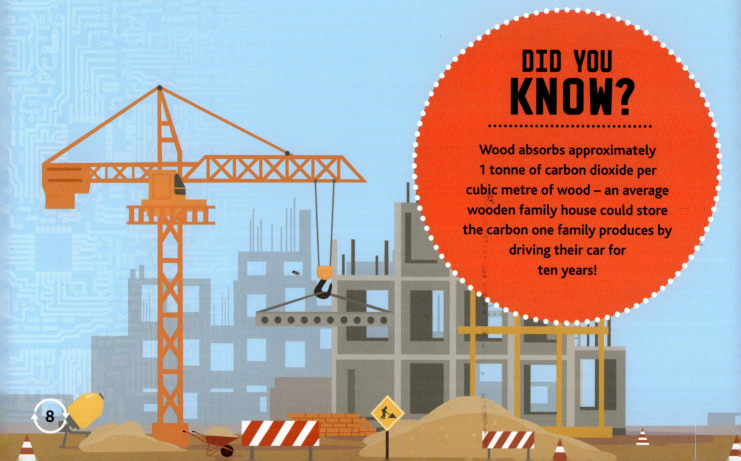

DID YOU KNOW?

Wood absorbs approximately 1 tonne of carbon dioxide per cubic metre of wood – an average wooden family house could store the carbon one family produces by driving their car for ten years!

LIVING MATERIALS

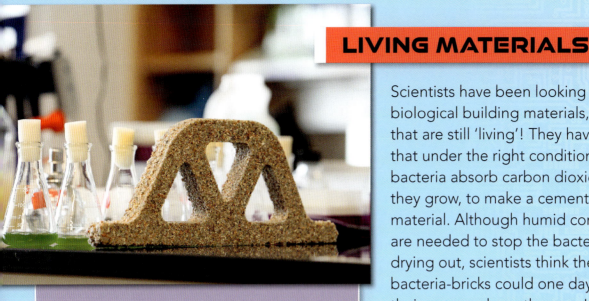

Living concrete can be 'grown' in a laboratory and moulded into different shapes.

Scientists have been looking at other biological building materials, ones that are still 'living'! They have found that under the right conditions, bacteria absorb carbon dioxide as they grow, to make a cement-like material. Although humid conditions are needed to stop the bacteria drying out, scientists think these bacteria-bricks could one day heal their own cracks as they age!

LOCAL SOLUTIONS

Scientists are also using emissions from local power plants to create a form of limestone. By taking the flue gases and bubbling them through salty water, the carbon dioxide (CO_2) combines with calcium from waste concrete to create calcium carbonate ($CaCO_3$) or limestone. The limestone rocks can then be used in new concrete. This method cuts down power plant emissions, but also reduces the mining and transportation of natural limestone.

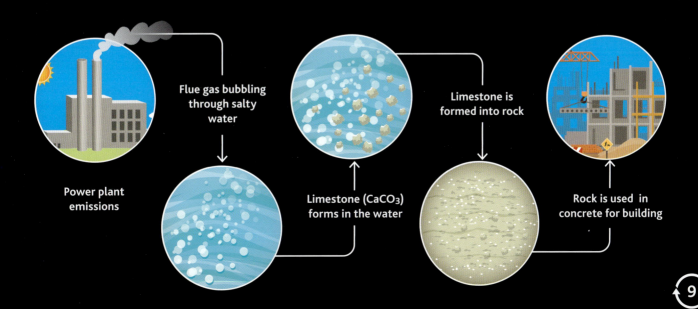

Power plant emissions → Flue gas bubbling through salty water → Limestone ($CaCO_3$) forms in the water → Limestone is formed into rock → Rock is used in concrete for building

SMART HOMES

Once our homes and workplaces are built, we need energy to light, power, heat and cool them. This energy produces about 20 per cent of the world's carbon emissions, although lifestyle changes and technology are helping to lower this figure.

EFFICIENT LIGHTING

New types of light bulbs have helped to cut our energy use. LED lights, for example, use up to 80 per cent less energy than older incandescent bulbs. Smart sensors can help to make even more savings (see diagram below).

HEAT AND POWER

Smart technology can also control our heating and power supplies (see diagram). Monitors can show the energy use and costs of individual appliances, with tips on how to make savings.

Energy management system monitors and controls the power consumption of lights, appliances, heating and air conditioning.

Lights are programmed to switch on when it gets dark (or when someone enters a room), and their brightness can be controlled individually.

Smart air conditioning works when the background temperature rises. It switches off when a window opens or if no one is at home.

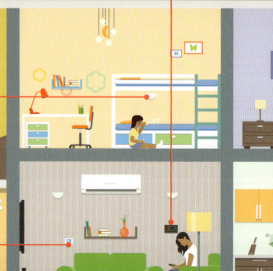

SAVING ENERGY

Did you know that some electronic devices use 'phantom power' when they're turned off but still plugged into a socket? These include gadgets that use a remote control or those, such as microwaves, with a continuous digital clock display. You can save this energy by using a 'smart power strip' – this cuts the power supply if a device is left on standby, or when a device has finished charging.

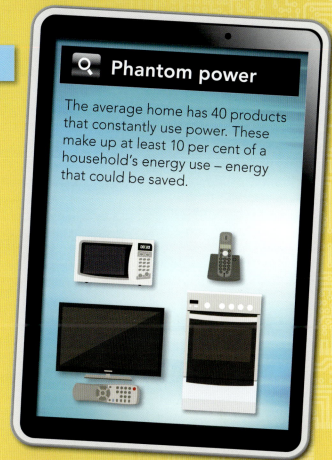

Phantom power

The average home has 40 products that constantly use power. These make up at least 10 per cent of a household's energy use – energy that could be saved.

Smart thermostats turn the heating on when the background temperature falls. Smart radiator valves know which rooms aren't used regularly.

Smart appliances turn 'off' when they're not in use and 'on' at particular times when there's plenty of energy going spare.

Smart bathroom appliances keep water flow and temperature at preferred settings.

SUPPLY AND DEMAND

Scientists are also using computer data to predict our behaviour. This 'artificial intelligence' can learn our daily routine. Instead of a constant supply, power can be produced to meet demand at certain times of day, generating fewer carbon emissions.

WATER WORLD

Earth's water cycle moves a constant supply of water, but we're using more water than ever, and can't create any more! Less than 3 per cent of Earth's water is fresh (not salty), and this isn't always accessible. Water has to be treated so we can use it to drink, cook, wash and make different products.

SAVING WATER

You'd be surprised how much water it takes to have a shower or run a bath. Smart meters encourage us to use less water at home, but it's important to remember that everything we eat, use, buy and wear also has a 'water footprint'. It takes about 125 litres of water to produce a single apple, for example.

An average bath uses 80 litres of water, while an eight-minute shower uses 60 litres.

MODERN APPLIANCES

In richer countries, the use of modern appliances such as dishwashers has increased average water use. Thankfully, green tech is helping to reduce the amount of water we use each day. Studies have shown that the latest dishwashers, for example, now use less water and energy than the 'running tap' method of washing up, which uses a steady stream of hot water.

Think twice before you wash and rinse!

SELF-CLEANING CLOTHES

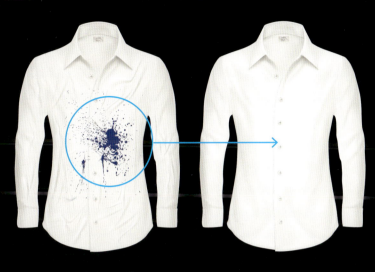

Science is helping to find new ways to keep our clothes clean.

To address the amount of water we're using to clean our clothes (a washing machine uses 50 litres per average wash), scientists have been developing textiles that clean themselves! They found that fabric covered with a thin layer of titanium oxide particles releases electrons when exposed to sunlight or artificial light. The electrons combine with oxygen molecules, enabling them to break down dirt and stains. The challenge now is to make this technology suitable for mass production.

Use at home

Toilet flushes use the most water at home. The average person flushes the toilet over 1,500 times a year!

- clothes washing 13%
- showers 12%
- baths and taps 21%
- other 5%
- drinking water 4%
- washing up 8%
- outdoor 7%
- toilet flushing 30%

DETECTING LEAKS

Around the world, more than 45 million cubic metres of water are lost every day due to faulty plumbing and leaky pipes. Scientists have been working on real-time leakage detection systems that raise the alarm as soon as a problem occurs. The water supply can be switched off remotely, preventing further loss until the problem is fixed.

CLOTHES AND FASHION

Many people throw away old clothes or buy things they never really wear – shopping habits that harm our planet. Textile production uses nearly 80 billion cubic metres of fresh water and releases 1.2 billion tonnes of carbon emissions a year, as well as transport and other costs.

FAST FASHION

Recent years have seen an increase in clothes consumption known as 'fast fashion'. Cheap clothes based on the latest trends are worn a few times until the fashion changes again. To slow things down, we need to change this behaviour. Buying fewer clothes that are longer-lasting (or buying second-hand clothes) reduces the need for new materials. It's better to mend clothes and to recycle things that can't be worn again. Sharing, swapping or renting clothes is also becoming more popular.

The clothing industry releases more than 10 per cent of the world's carbon emissions each year.

DIFFERENT FABRICS

Producing artificial fabrics (such as polyester) uses more energy than producing plant-based fibres (such as hemp). Artificial fabrics aren't biodegradable because they're a type of plastic (see page 20), and some contain microfibres that pollute water when they're washed. Scientists have been developing more eco-friendly fibres, such as tencel. Reusing the water and chemicals needed to extract them also saves on water and reduces pollution.

Tencel is a new fabric that comes from the eucalyptus tree, which can be grown in sustainable forests.

LIVE ORGANISMS

Scientists are also developing strong, flexible fibres from live organisms, such as bacteria, yeast and fungi! These biodegradable materials could be grown on smaller areas of land without using pesticides. They could also be grown to fit moulds, so less 'off-cut' material goes to waste. Scientists think the fabrics could even repair their own rips or tears!

DID YOU KNOW?

Over 500,000 tonnes of microfibres reach the oceans each year – the equivalent of more than 50 billion plastic bottles.

This laser machine cuts fabrics, but waste material is left behind. New fabrics could be grown to exact shapes.

FEEDING THE WORLD

We have over 7 billion people to feed, but a rich minority use far more food resources than the rest. Food production uses about 30 per cent of our energy and creates about 30 per cent of carbon emissions. It also uses a lot of fresh water and land.

CITY FARMS

As Earth's climate warms, our crops are at risk. 'Indoor vertical farms' are one way to create a sustainable food supply in cities. By stacking plants on top of each other in a controlled environment, these farms produce crops in a limited space, and avoid transportation costs to another location because they feed city residents. They also use up to 70 per cent less water than traditional farms.

Could vertical farms be the food of the future for city dwellers?

SMART EQUIPMENT

Drones and sensors can monitor soil conditions on a large traditional farm and find diseased or damaged crops. Robots and automated tractors can help with planting, watering and harvesting. The use of data and artificial intelligence can also help farmers to predict future conditions and grow crops more successfully.

SHOPPING HABITS

Meat and dairy farming use over 80 per cent of the world's farmland and create 60 per cent of agriculture's emissions (cows produce a lot of methane, for example, mainly through belching!). We can help by eating more plant-based foods. Local, seasonal foods (that don't require heated greenhouses) have no need to be transported. Apps can help shoppers to make smarter choices, using data from food labels or shopping receipts to estimate the environmental impact of different foods.

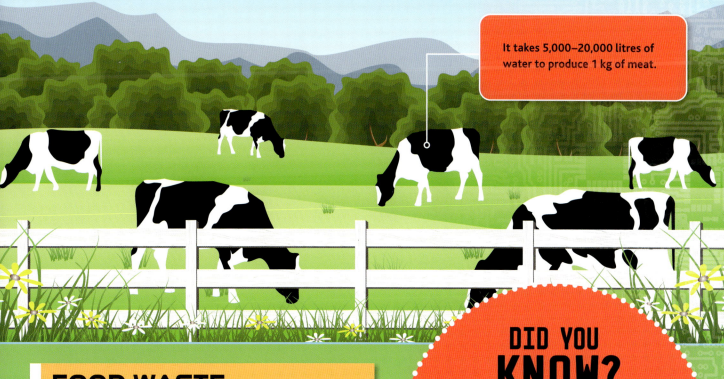

It takes 5,000–20,000 litres of water to produce 1 kg of meat.

FOOD WASTE

About a third of the food we produce is currently wasted (or lost through spoilage). If food waste enters landfill, it releases harmful methane (see page 23). We can reduce waste by watching out for sell-by dates and only buying or serving what we need. Technology can also make our supply systems more efficient. For example, new apps advertise leftover food from shops and restaurants or 'imperfect' produce such as wonky fruit and vegetables, to be sold at a reduced price.

DID YOU KNOW?

If every week, families in the UK changed one red-meat-based meal for a plant-based meal, over the course of a year it would reduce the same carbon footprint as taking 16 million cars off the road!

PACKAGING AND PARCELS

Our food is packaged to stay fresh, our toiletries come in bottles and cans, and we're shopping online more than ever. Packaging needs to be reusable to save Earth's resources. We can all use a 'bag for life' or a reusable coffee cup, but can we do more?

PLANT-BASED MATERIALS

Most packaging, such as cardboard, can be recycled. But recycling uses a lot of energy (see page 22). Suppliers are turning to biodegradable packaging made from plant-based fibres. Sugarcane and coconut husks can be used for packaging and cartons (see right), and mushroom-based packaging used to protect delicate goods.

EDIBLE PACKAGING

To help reduce waste, some packaging can now be eaten or composted. For example, sweet or cupcake wrappers made from rice or potato starch, dissolvable sachets made from seaweed, and party cups made from a seaweed-based gelatin that taste like jelly! Adding ingredients to packaging (see left) is another way to reduce the materials we use, if the packaging is composted in the correct manner.

Ingredients are printed in the packaging of this compostable plant-based cup so you just add water to make an energy drink.

DRONE DELIVERIES

An increase in online shopping has meant more home deliveries, raising fuel consumption and carbon emissions. In the future, robots or drones could deliver our packages for us. While drones are currently good at getting supplies to remote areas, scientists are looking at ways to improve the cost, safety, security and accuracy of delivering packages in busy cities.

Drone deliveries could reduce transportation costs, but more research is needed into their safety and security.

SMART SOLUTIONS

To cut down on food waste (see page 17), smart packaging can record more reliable 'best before' dates so food isn't wasted unnecessarily. One designer has proposed a gel-filled label that starts to create bumps on the packaging when the food inside becomes unsafe to eat. Plastic labels on fruit and vegetables can also be replaced with laser technology that harmlessly marks the skin.

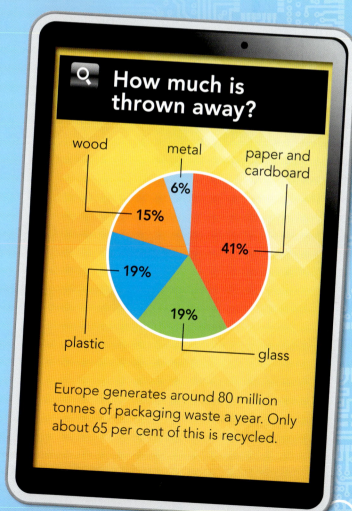

How much is thrown away?

- paper and cardboard: 41%
- glass: 19%
- plastic: 19%
- wood: 15%
- metal: 6%

Europe generates around 80 million tonnes of packaging waste a year. Only about 65 per cent of this is recycled.

WORKING WITH PLASTIC

Plastic is a hot topic and companies worldwide are trying to reduce the amount of plastic in their packaging. Using plastic is a hygienic way to keep food fresher for longer, but it doesn't break down when thrown away and is polluting our land and oceans.

There are an estimated 17,760 pieces of plastic in every square kilometre of ocean.

SAFER RECYCLING

Many plastics can be recycled using chemicals, machines or heat. But these processes use a lot of energy and cause pollution themselves. Although we can try to avoid using single-use plastics, such as straws and water bottles, we still need to deal with the plastics that have already been produced. Scientists are developing a way to use bacteria to digest plastic and turn it into an eco-friendly material that can be recycled easily or used as a building material.

DID YOU KNOW?

Since 1950, we've produced an estimated 8.3 billion tonnes of plastic, of which we have thrown away 6.3 billion tonnes! Nearly 80 per cent of this waste has ended up in landfill or has been found in our environment.

REUSABLE RESOURCES

In 2019, scientists discovered a new plastic polymer called PDK (Polydiketoenamine). They found it could be recycled again and again without losing its strength. If PDK was used for new plastic products, less plastic would need to be made.

Scientists had another breakthrough in 2019 when they realised waste plastic could be turned into chemicals and used to generate electricity. The plastic could be recycled without using fossil fuels or producing carbon emissions, although the process was only carried out on a small scale.

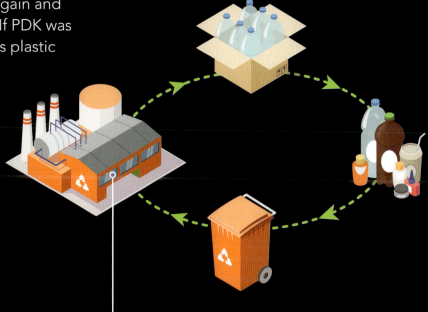

Finding more efficient ways to recycle the plastic we already have can help to reduce plastic levels in the future.

ALTERNATIVE PLASTICS

Plant-based plastics are one solution for takeaway cups and containers. These can now be made from materials such as sugar, agar (seaweed) and mycelium (found in fungi) (see page 18). Film wrapping can be made from a milk protein that is edible, printable and biodegradable. It also keeps out oxygen 500 times more efficiently than traditional plastic film.

Scientists tested their milk-protein film as packaging for blocks of cheese.

WASTE AND RECYCLING

We should always try to reduce or reuse the things we have, before recycling or throwing them away. The recycling process uses a lot of energy, as well as producing carbon emissions. Our household waste goes to landfill or is burned, causing further emissions.

SEPARATING WASTE

A new invention called the VolCat (volatile catalyst) cleans and separates materials for recycling in a hot pressurised oven, removing the need to wash and sort them first. Although VolCat uses energy, it means more complex materials can be recycled, too.

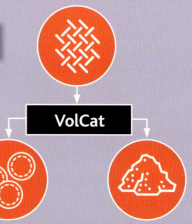

The VolCat can break down a cotton/polyester blend of fabric into a ball of cotton fibres and polyester powder.

SMART BINS

Some 'smart bins' use image recognition and artificial intelligence to identify materials and separate them for recycling. Others use solar power to compress the waste and a signal is sent when the bin needs emptying. In some countries, smart bins identify and track recycling habits, and consumers are charged a fee for un-recycled waste.

This smart recycling bin uses image recognition to light up the correct chute.

TACKLING E-WASTE

With technology developing all the time, electronic waste is a big problem. About 50 million tonnes is generated each year (the same as throwing away 1,000 laptops a second!). E-waste contains toxic chemicals, such as lead and mercury. Scientists have been finding ways to make circuit boards that dissolve in water after use, and ways to use bacteria to extract the different metals.

LANDFILL CLEAN-UP

Rotting waste in landfill is a source of methane emissions – a greenhouse gas 28 times more harmful than carbon dioxide. Scientists have been looking at ways to turn this methane into electricity. Tubes collect the gas, which is then compressed. The heat generated is used to boil water to power a steam turbine and generate electricity. Methane gas can also be used as a biofuel or converted into hydrogen gas to power vehicles as part of a fuel cell.

Our increased reliance on computers, mobile phones and smart technology means that e-waste recycling is more important than ever.

Landfills release 12 per cent of the world's methane emissions.

DID YOU KNOW?

Every year, over 2 billion tonnes of household waste is produced globally – more than 60 tonnes of waste a second! For every bag of waste, about 70 bags has been generated earlier to create the products that are now waste.

GETTING AROUND

With increased demand for global travel, as well as the import and export of different products, transport emissions are on the rise. Transport by road, rail, sea and air releases over 24 per cent of global carbon emissions, mainly to fulfil the demands of richer nations.

REDUCING EMISSIONS

Walking, cycling, car-sharing and taking public transport are good ways to reduce the number of cars on our roads and the emissions they release. Keeping a car well maintained, with properly inflated tyres can also mean it uses less fuel. For longer journeys, taking trains instead of planes is preferable. Navigation apps can now show us the 'carbon cost' of a trip, so we can make an informed choice about our journeys.

Studies show that travelling from London to Paris by train instead of plane reduces the journey's carbon emissions by 91 per cent!

GOING ELECTRIC

Electric cars could mean far lower carbon emissions, as long as their batteries are charged with renewable energy. The challenge is to make these cars more affordable and to improve their batteries. Scientists are currently working on a 'supercapacitor' that could be up to 10,000 times more powerful than existing car batteries, allowing cars to travel further between charges and fully recharge in a few minutes.

MAINTAINING ROADS

Keeping roads in good shape improves vehicles' efficiency, helping to lower emissions. Some road surfaces are now made from recycled plastic as it doesn't degrade. Studies have shown that growing trees alongside busy, populated roads can help to filter harmful particles from the air. The leaves absorb and store some of the pollution, which is then washed away by the rain.

Trees alongside a busy school road can help to absorb emissions from cars and buses.

TRAVEL AND TOURISM

It's important that we cut down on air travel, unnecessary trips and planes that fly with empty seats. In the future, planes could be powered by a newly developed jet fuel that uses industrial waste gases and lowers emissions by 50–70 per cent. Bacteria are used to turn the gases into ethanol (alcohol), which can be converted into a liquid fuel.

DID YOU KNOW?

Technology can bring a taste of tourism, without the need to travel. You can experience the sights, sounds and senses of climbing Mount Everest, for example, from the comfort of your own home, using a virtual reality headset.

SMART CITIES

Today, over 55 per cent of people worldwide live in cities, and this figure is expected to reach nearly 70 per cent by 2050. Scientists have been looking at ways to make our city spaces cleaner and less polluting, and to help city dwellers live in a more eco-friendly way.

GETTING CONNECTED

The Internet has revolutionised our world, and its uses are multiplying. 'The Internet of Things' describes the way different devices can connect to the Internet and share information. Traffic light sensors, for example, can keep traffic moving. Drivers can be alerted to their nearest parking spot or car-charging station. Waste can be collected only when the bins are nearly full. The opportunities are endless!

Traffic light sensors help to ease congestion, which in turn prevents the build-up of fumes.

DID YOU KNOW?

Smart-city solutions could reduce carbon emissions by up to 15 per cent, solid waste by up to 130 kg per person per year, and up to 80 litres of water per person per day.

TRANSFORMING DUBAI

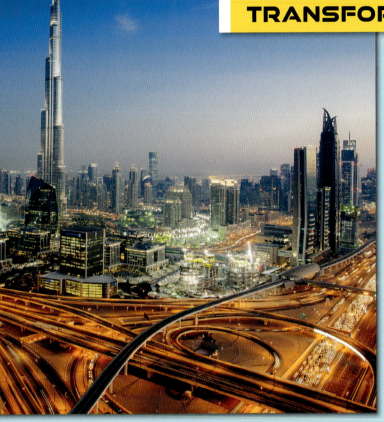

Many cities around the world are striving to improve their energy efficiency and to reduce emissions. In 2013, for example, the United Arab Emirates (UAE) announced the 'Smart Dubai Initiative' to make the city more sustainable. Dubai now has electric-car charging stations, smart parking systems, traffic monitoring, smart energy meters and a smart power grid to regulate energy supplies.

CLEVER CANALS

In Amsterdam, the world's first robotic boats are being developed to transform the city and its 165 canals. These 'roboats' have cameras and sensors to collect data. If the city's streets become too busy, the boats form floating bridges or stages that can temporarily ease congestion. With satellite navigation and sensors, they can find the shortest route from A to B, and avoid traffic in their path.

Amsterdam's roboats will be used 'on-demand' to transport people and goods, and to collect waste.

SUSTAINABLE DEVELOPMENT

Poorer countries have a lower carbon footprint than richer ones, but how can they improve living standards in an eco-friendly way? Technology is helping to bridge the gap with the sharing of ideas as well as past mistakes.

PARTNERS WORLDWIDE

Richer countries have a responsibility to share knowledge with countries seeking to catch up. Technology can connect key people in an international development project, helping to combine local knowledge with hi-tech solutions, such as loaning expensive farming machinery to those in need.

RELIABLE POWER

In India, many poor rural communities don't have access to affordable, reliable electricity. Their only source of reliable power is a polluting diesel generator. A new project is aiming to build 10,000 solar microgrids to power nearly 5 million Indian homes. Each year this will cut 1 million tonnes of carbon emissions and 57 million litres of diesel.

The electricity produced by solar microgrids in India will have a huge impact on local jobs, farming, education and healthcare.

SHARING KNOWLEDGE

In Kenya and Tanzania, technology is revolutionising the lives of farmers. Rural farmers can be isolated due to poorly maintained roads and the problem of a global language barrier. Text-based services reach farmers with a mobile phone (but no Internet access). They can order seeds and fertilisers by text and any questions are answered using artificial intelligence.

For farmers with Internet access, weather updates, subtitled videos on farming techniques and access to an online marketplace are all improving efficiency.

🔍 Innovative ideas

In 2019, Anna Luísa Beserra from Brazil was named a 'Young Champion of the Earth' by the United Nations. Her idea of using the Sun's energy to kill harmful bacteria in rain water, making it safe to drink, really inspired the judges!

LAST WORD

Of course, technology isn't the only answer to our problems. The Internet uses around 10 per cent of the world's electricity consumption, for example. But it's helping us to see a way forward. So many green tech ideas have taken their inspiration from the wonders of nature – trees, rocks and bacteria that absorb carbon, and living organisms that reproduce rapidly. If we can make changes to the way we live and use technology to help us tap into Earth's natural ability to heal, there is great hope for the future.

GLOSSARY

automated something that works automatically, with minimum human input

biodegradable material that breaks down naturally into the soil or water

biofuel fuel made from plant material, animal waste or captured methane gas

carbon footprint amount of emissions released as the result of an activity

data information, facts and figures collected and used to better understand something

drone unmanned flying device that can be controlled from a distance, or using sensors and satellite navigation

electrons tiny particles charged with electrical energy, found inside small particles called atoms

emissions substances – typically harmful, polluting gases – released into the air

flue gases mixture of gases produced when a substance is burned

fossil fuel natural fuel, such as oil, that takes millions of years to form and can be burned for energy or heat

fresh water naturally occurring water that is not salty

fuel cell battery that uses the chemical energy of a fuel to produce electricity

greenhouse gas gas that traps the Sun's heat in Earth's atmosphere, warming our planet

incandescent bulb light bulb that glows when a wire inside it becomes hot

microfibres tiny artificial fibres used in some fabrics

microgrid small-scale power grid that generates electricity

molecule group of two or more small particles, called atoms, that make a particular substance

organism living thing of any kind

pesticides substances used to destroy insects or other living things that might damage crops

polymer big molecule made up of small repeating units

sustainable a way of doing things that can continue for a long time. For example, a sustainable use of Earth's resources

thermostat device that regulates the temperature of a system

FURTHER INFORMATION

BOOKS

Eco Works: How Carbon Footprints Work
by Nick Hunter (Franklin Watts)
Learn what makes up someone's carbon footprint and what we can do to reduce it.

Putting the Planet First: Eco-cities
by Nancy Dickmann (Wayland)
From recycling drinking water to green transport links, find out how cities are becoming more sustainable.

This Book is Not Rubbish
by Isabel Thomas (Wren & Rook)
Discover how saving the planet is not as difficult as you think.

VIDEOS

How a Family of 5 Make Almost Zero Waste
youtube.com/watch?v=B5ijPk5_8pM
The inspiring story of a waste-free family from Hobart, Australia.

Climate Friendly Living – Eco Eye series 15
youtube.com/watch?v=t_EI1FUD4Ns
Dr Lara Dungan learns about her own carbon footprint and how to minimise its impact.

5 Eco-Friendly Building Materials
youtube.com/watch?v=NrQOZfMEXeQ
Discover how buildings of the future could change, and why LEGO® skills are more important than you think!

INDEX

artificial intelligence 11, 16, 22, 29

bacteria 9, 15, 20, 23, 25, 29

buildings 4, 8–9, 20

carbon dioxide 6, 8, 9, 23

carbon footprint 6, 7, 8, 9, 17, 24, 28

cities 16, 19, 26–27

climate change 4, 16

clothes 4, 12, 13, 14–15

data 11, 16, 17, 27

development 4, 5, 28–29

Earth Overshoot Day 5

emissions 6, 8, 9, 10, 11, 14, 16, 17, 19, 21, 22, 23, 24, 25, 26, 28

energy 5, 6–7, 10–11, 12, 15, 16, 18, 20, 22, 24, 27, 28, 29

farming 16, 17, 28, 29

food 4, 12, 16–17, 18, 19, 20

fossil fuels 6, 21, 28

greenhouse gases (see emissions)

homes 6, 7, 10–11, 12, 13, 19, 25, 28

packaging 18–19, 20, 21

plastic 15, 19, 20–21, 25

pollution 4, 5, 6, 8, 15, 20, 25, 26, 28

population 4, 16, 26

recycling 14, 18, 19, 20, 21, 22–23, 25

resources 4, 5, 6, 7, 18, 21, 22, 24, 28
 non-renewable 6, 21, 28
 renewable 6–7, 24

shopping 14, 17, 18, 19

transport 4, 8, 9, 14, 16, 17, 19, 22, 24–25, 27

waste 6, 9, 15, 17, 18, 19, 20, 21, 22–23, 25, 26, 27

water 6, 9, 11, 12–13, 14, 15, 16, 17, 18, 20, 23, 26, 29